How To Play Disc Golf

A Beginner's Guide to Learn the Disc Golf Rules, Etiquette, Equipment, and Proper Technique

By: Roger Banks

Text Copyright © Lightbulb Publishing

All rights reserved. No part of this guide may be reproduced in any form without permission in writing from the publisher except in the case of brief quotations embodied in critical articles or reviews.

Legal & Disclaimer

The information contained in this book and its contents is not designed to replace or take the place of any form of medical or professional advice; and is not meant to replace the need for independent medical, financial, legal or other professional advice or services, as may be required. The content and information in this book has been provided for educational and entertainment purposes only.

The content and information contained in this book has been compiled from sources deemed reliable, and it is accurate to the best of the Author's knowledge, information, and belief. However, the Author cannot guarantee its accuracy and validity and cannot be held liable for any errors and/or omissions. Further, changes are periodically made to this book as and when needed. Where appropriate and/or necessary, you must consult a professional (including but not limited to your doctor, attorney, financial advisor or such other professional advisor) before using any of the suggested remedies, techniques, or information in this book.

Upon using the contents and information contained in this book, you agree to hold harmless the Author from and against any damages, costs, and expenses, including any legal fees potentially resulting from the application of any of the information provided by this book. This disclaimer applies to any loss, damages or injury caused by the use and application, whether directly or indirectly, of any advice or information presented, whether for breach of contract, tort, negligence, personal injury, criminal intent, or under any other cause of action.

You agree to accept all risks of using the information presented in this book.

You agree that by continuing to read this book, where appropriate and/or necessary, you shall consult a professional (including but not limited to your doctor, attorney, or financial advisor or such other advisor as needed) before using any of the suggested remedies, techniques, or information in this book.

Table of Contents

Chapter 1: Introduction 1

Chapter 2: Disc Beginner Setup 5

Chapter 3: Rules and Etiquettes of the Game 13

Chapter 4: Equipment 33

Chapter 5: How to Play the Game? 47

Chapter 6: Some More Pointers Before You Start Playing 53

Chapter 7: Physical Fitness and Safety Measures 61

Chapter 8: Tack Your Score 65

Chapter 9: Mental Well-Being 69

Chapter 10: Tips and Tricks of the Game for Beginners 73

Conclusion 79

Chapter 1
Introduction

Much like the regular game of golf, disc golf is played in a similar manner. Learning to play disc golf is an excellent way to while away to spend quality time with friends and family. You can even decide to go professional with it if you desire. With this book, you can learn everything you need about playing disc golf. It does not matter whether you have little to no knowledge about how to play the sport. And if you have experience with the game, this book will also provide some valuable tips to help you improve. But before we jump right into it, let's go back to where it all began.

History of Disc Golf

Like every sport we play, disc golf has a fascinating history of how it spread around the world. The origin of disc golf dates back to the 1900s when the first game was played in Bladworth, Saskatchewan, Canada, in 1927. The game was played by a group of Elementary School buddies throwing tin lids into a 4 feet wide circle in the school fields. Back then, the game was called the Tin Lid Golf. Everyone seemed so captivated by the game that it became a regular sport. Soon, words began to spread, and more people began participating in the sport.

Later in the 1960s, the game was modernized, although there are controversies about who came up with the idea first. The consensus is that multiple people independently played it throughout the 1960s. For example, in 1964, students at Rice University in Huston,

Texas, held disc golf tournaments with trees as their target. Also, in the early 1960s, players at Augusta, Georgia, played disc golf by tossing Frisbees into a 50-gallon barrel trash can. The list continues, making it quite hard to pinpoint where its modernization began.

But this controversy ended with two pioneers of the game, Dave Dunipace and Steady Ed Headrick, two players and inventors. In 1976, Steady Ed Headrick formalized the rules of the game as well as founded the Recreational Disc Golf Association (RDGA), Professional Disc Golf Association (PDGA), and the Disc Golf Association (DGA). Fast forward to 1983, Dave Dunipace designed the first formal disc golf target that we all know today. The diagram below is the design of Dave's disc golf target.

Understanding the Game

Disc golf, as we said earlier, is a game played like regular golf, but instead of targeting a cup on the floor as with regular golf, in disc golf, the target is a net hung on a short pole. The game is played with a disc, which has varying types. The disc is commonly made with a polypropene plastic material. However, you can find them in

Introduction

varying types of other materials. Each disc in the game has a number on it that indicates the intended flight. As a beginner, it helps to practice with a low-speed disc and work your way to a high-speed one.

To play the game, the player stands far from the net target. The area where the player stands to throw the disc is called the tee pad. From the tee pad, the player throws the disc at the target to complete within 9 or 18 throws to win. When a player throws the disc, wherever it lands, he/she continues to throw from that spot in the next throw until it reaches the basket. The number of throws a player uses to get the disc into the basket is usually tailed. To win the game, you must aim to get the disc into the basket with the lowest number of total throws.

Understanding the game of disc golf is pretty easy and exciting. This book will guide you on playing disc golf, from knowing nothing about the game to playing straight after reading it. There will also be lots of diagrams and images to better illustrate everything about playing disc golf.

Chapter 2
Disc Beginner Setup

To some people, playing disc golf is all about throwing a disc into a net. However, to throw a disc, players have to use certain techniques. If not, you will simply be throwing the disc randomly with little to no success, causing you to lose every time you play with someone who understands the game a little more than you. If you want to play this game, there are a few basic setups you need to know, such as how to hold the disc, how to throw it, and factors that can impact your throw, amongst others. In this book chapter, you will learn all that with a few tips.

Factors that Influence Your Throw

There are a couple of factors you need to be aware of that can influence the outcome of your throw. Knowing how these factors influence your throw can help you immensely develop your disc playing skills by being cautious of them. Below are some of the most common factors that influence your throw many beginners struggle with:

- **Arm speed/power**

    While the disc player throw in the disc golf game is not heavy, you need to build your muscles to possess the right speed and power level to throw the disc adequately. Knowing your arm power and speed will help you know which category to compete in, so you don't go beyond your capacity when you are not yet ready. For example, if player A can throw a disc with a maximum distance of 250m, it is improbable they will be able to compete in a match with a 350m rating.

- **Technique**

  The technique you are using to throw the disc will also impact how far you throw. People use several techniques to throw a disc in disc golf, such as the forehand throw or backhand throw. You can use your left or right hands to get a more powerful throw. Note that if the technique you use is not right for you, it will influence throw negatively. For example, if you are right-handed but throw with your left hand, you will most likely perform woefully.

- **Release angle**

  The angle you release the disc is another thing to take into consideration. When you don't have good timing for the release handle, the flight path of your disc will not be as you intended. Hence, you should strongly work on your release angle to better target the basket. Learn more about throwing styles to improve your release angle.

- **Plastic-type**

  As we said earlier, disc golf discs are made of varying types of plastic. The type of plastic used on your disc can influence your throw by impacting the speed and flight path. Discs made with less durable plastic are less stable flight paths. As a rule of thumb, aim to own a premium plastic disc for a more stable flight.

- **Disc weight**

    The weight of the disc you use can influence the speed/power of your throw. When the disc is heavier, it will require more effort to throw at an adequate distance. Note that throwing the disc with more power means it will have a lower High Speed Turn (HST) value, with a more distance traveled and curving travel path. Whereas disc throws with less power will have a higher HST value, with less distance traveled and curving travel path and distance.

- **Disc condition**

    It is also helpful to take note of the condition of the disc. Several factors can influence the condition of the disc. For example, the disc could deteriorate due to heavy usage with cracks and bends. The condition of the disc can impact the shape, which influences the travel path when you throw it. It is always a good idea to change the disc periodically.

Grip Types

Now that you know what can influence your throw let us talk a bit about how you can grip the disc. There are two main types of grips: the backhand and the forehand. As a beginner, you must take note of the different types of grips to know what works best for you. Each type of grip works best for a particular type of throw. Knowing when to apply a type of grip for the throw you are about to take will help you achieve the lowest cumulative number of throws. Below is a list of the different grips you can use in disc golf.

Backhand grips

- Power grip

- Fan grip

- Modified power grip

- Modified fan grip

Forehand grips

- Split grip

- Stacked grip

- Power grip

Throwing Styles

There are different mechanics to throwing disc golf, but your success in landing the disc in the basket has a lot to do with how you hold the disc. A disc golf player should be able to throw the disc several meters and sink it in the basket. This may seem almost overwhelming for a beginner, but it is possible. One way to improve your throwing skill is to learn the different throwing styles in the sport. Whether you are a seasoned player or a veteran, understanding the different throwing styles will go a long way in helping you put better. Here's a list of the different throwing styles you can use in disc golf:

- Backhand
- Forehand
- Hyzer
- Anhyzer
- Turnover shot
- Roller shot
- S shot
- Hyzer flip
- Flex shot
- Thumber and tomahawk shots

Factors that Impact Your Throw

Stopping becomes quite difficult when you get into the excitement of understanding disc golf. While the whole learning process is exhilarating, it's important to note that some factors can impact your throw. Below are some common factors that can impact your throw:

- **Improper foot placement**

It all begins with a good stance when you want to throw the disc. If your stance does not correlate with your throwing style and grip, it will make your throw inefficient. There are several stances in disc throwing most popular are the X-step, the brace, and shifting your weight from the left to the right and vice versa.

- **Wind resistant**

    Another thing that can impact your throw is wind resistance. Due to the disc's lightweight nature, it is greatly affected by the wind. The disc wouldn't travel far when you throw against the wind, especially when the current is high. Similarly, when you throw the disc in the direction of a high wind current, though it may travel farther this time, but it would have very little accuracy. In other to get the most out of your throw, It is always important to take note of the direction of the wind

- **Wrong disc**

    As we mentioned earlier, there are different types of discs. Each disc in disc golf differs in speed, accuracy, and control. Typically, they all range between 8 and 9 inches in diameter and weigh between 150 and 180 grams. Of the wide variety of discs in the market, they can all be categorized into three main groups, the drivers, all-purpose mid-range discs, and putters. Using a putter disc for a throw, you are meant to use the driver disc for that will greatly impact your throw.

- **Throwing power**

    Lastly, the amount of power you put into throwing the disc is a crucial factor that impacts the throw. Using too much or inadequate power than required would greatly influence how far the disc will travel. Using too much power may give you much distance, but with little accuracy. Whereas using inadequate power may let you have more accuracy but less distance. To use the right amount of power, practice more on your gripping strength as it plays a crucial role in a disc golf game.

Suitable Distance for Beginners to Throw Disc Golf

An important thing every beginner disc golf player should take note of is their throwing distance. According to the Professional Disc Golf Association, the average distance expected for beginners to throw a disc is between 175 and 250 feet. As they advance in the sport, their throwing distance should increase by an average of 20%. After about 1 to 2 years, the average throwing distance should increase to approximately 200 to 300 feet. And after 2 to 3 years, the average throwing distance should increase to 250 to 350 feet. Advanced disc golf players have a disc throwing distance of 450 feet.

Chapter 3
Rules and Etiquettes of the Game

In every game of sport, there are rules guiding the game. These rules bound the game together, making it easy to know who is winning and losing. The golden rule of disc golf is to have the lowest number of throws to win. Understanding the rules and etiquette of disc golf will help you become a better player.

To help you be a better player, we complied with this chapter with the basic rules you need to know about the game. So, by the end of this chapter, you will have an in-depth knowledge of how to hold and throw discs in disc golf. You would also learn the game's guidelines and how to play the game. So, let's get right into it.

How to Play the Game?

Disc golf is a similar game to the traditional golf game. However, unlike using a golf club and ball to aim for a hole, disc golf involves using a disc and aiming for a disc golf basket. The game's objective is to throw the disc golf into the basket with the fewest number of throws. Each throw starts from a tee area and finishes with the disc landing in the basket. Most of the time, the course can include 9 or 18 holes. So, players start from the first hole and try to complete the course with the fewest number of throws, playing through to the last hole.

The tee-off order of who to take the first tee is decided by an agreement or by flipping discs. After determining who should be in the first tee order, the subsequent tee-off order is determined by scores of previous holes. The player with the lowest scores tees off first. For each throw, a mini marker disc is used to determine the lie (where the disc came to rest). The mini marker disc is a small disc that is not used to play but complies with the professional disc golf association (PDGA) Technical Standards for mini marker disc. And the thrown disc is always left on the lie until the marker is used to mark it.

When throwing the disc golf, proper positioning is important, although it requires some practice. When throwing, the foot you put your weight on can greatly impact your throw. The plant foot or the foot you put your weight on should be as close to the front line as reasonable as possible. In no case should your leg be ahead of the line or be a foot behind the line. At the same time, the other foot can be placed anywhere as long as it is no closer to the hole than the rear of the marker disc.

Stepping past the marker disc after a throw is allowed on any throw except for when you are putting (throwing where the rear of the marker disc is within 10 meters of the hole). It is not allowed to fall forward in other to keep your balance after a putting shot.

If the disc gets stuck in a tree or bush, a marker is placed directly beneath it, and the disc is carefully removed from the tree. If the disc should go out of bounds, you will be penalized with an extra throw. Also, you will be penalized with an extra throw if this should happen. Some courses have out-of-bound areas, so do well to keep out of them. Water hazards are also to be avoided because it attracts an extra one-throw penalty to your throws. Standing water or mud on the main course caused by sprinklers is not considered out of bounds.

Rules and Etiquettes of the Game

Players must be kept out of alternate-use areas in some courses to make the course more challenging. In such courses, it is normally designated on the tee sign. The arrow indicates the side and direction the disc must pass. If the disc should pass the wrong side of the mandated area, you will be penalized to re-throw from the previous lie from a designated drop zone area, which comes with a one-throw penalty.

At the end of the course, the player with the lowest total cumulative throws wins. Note that disc golf can be played in so many types of terrain. And sometimes, lands that may not be suitable for other park activities may be the perfect terrain for a disc golf course. Disc golf may be one of the best fitness sports. It is a healthy activity, easy to learn, and playable by everyone of all ages and fitness levels. If you can throw a Frisbee, then you can play disc golf.

How to Hold a Disc Golf Disc?

You can hold the disc in a golf disc in many different ways. How you hold the disc ultimately depends on whether you are driving, approaching, or putting. As mentioned in the previous chapter, holding disc can also vary if you throw backhand or forehand. Backhand throws are often the most basic and suited for beginner players, while forehands are more suited for intermediate and advanced players. In this book section, we will be looking at some of the most common types of grips that any beginners can start with and master.

Backhand grips

As you probably can already tell, the backhand grip is a type of grip where your hand curls over the disc with your palm resting on the top of the flight plate. You should know four main types of backhand grips: power grip, fan grip, modified power grip, and modified fan grip. Let's take a look at their difference below:

- **Power grip**

The power grip is a type of grip that lets you put the maximum amount of power on the disc without worrying much about slipping too early. The power grip is ideal when going for a tee shot. However, it is not all that great for a shot that requires high accuracy. The power grip is performed by holding the disc firmly in the middle of your palm with your thumb on the rim of the disc, your fingers curled around the edge, and the tips set inside the rim of the bottom of the disc.

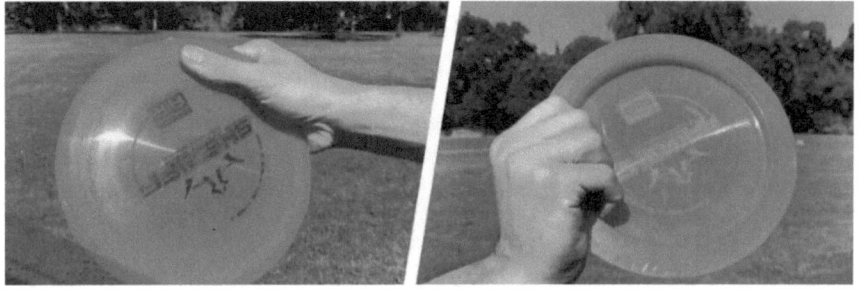

- **Fan grip**

The fan grip is a type of grip that provides you with the highest degree of accuracy and control. However, with this grip, you would have to sacrifice covering much distance for more control. This grip is ideal for taking the putting shot. The fan grip is performed by holding the disc in your dominant hand with your fingers splayed out and resting on the bottom of the disc.

- **Modified power grip**

The modified power grip is similar to the power grip. However, it is a type of grip to go for when you want to achieve power, accuracy, and distance. You may have to sacrifice a bit of distance with this type of grip, but the extra accuracy makes it all worthwhile. To perform the modified power grip, hold the disc with your fingers splayed out slightly around the edge to rest on the inside lid, giving your forefingers enough space to wrap around the outside edge of the disc.

- **Modified fan grip**

The modified fan grip, on the other hand, offers you a high degree of accuracy but with a bit more distance. To perform this grip, hold the disc with your pinky and forefinger curled around the outside while your ring finger and middle finger curls around the outside of the disc. This type of grip is great when taking a midrange shot. Depending on the situation, you can use this type of grip for fairway driving or an approaching shot.

Forehand grips

The other main type of grips you should use is the forehand grips which allow you to take every kind of shot like fairway driving, driving off the tee, midrange shots, and so on. The only shot you may find difficult with these grips is probably putting. You should know three main types of forehand grips: split grip, stacked grip, and power grip. Let's talk about them below:

- **Split grip**

The split-grip is the best forehand grip that gives you the most accuracy. It is similar to the fan grip in the backhand grip we talked about earlier. To perform this grip, hold the disc with your forefinger, and middle finger spread out on the bottom and your thumb on top. Your middle finger should rest along the inner lips, while your ring finger and pinky rest on the outside lip of the disc for support.

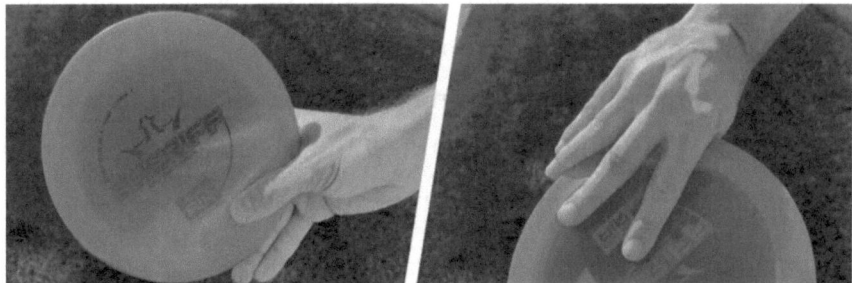

- **Stacked grip**

The stacked grip is great for good balance and power for better accuracy and more distance to cover. With this grip, you can use more power in your swing without losing much control. To perform this grip, hold the disc with your middle and forefinger stacked on top of each other and your thumb on top. Your ring finger and pinky finger should stay on the outside lip of the disc for support.

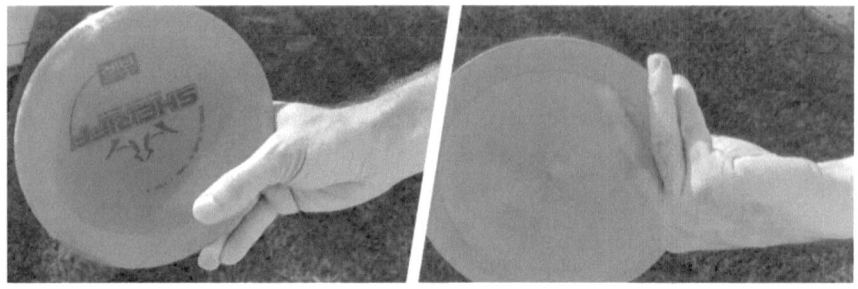

- **Power grip**

The power grip is a forehand grip that lets you maximize your distance potential. Hold the disc in your dominant hand between your forefingers and thumb to perform this grip. Your thumb is placed on the top of the plate, and your forefinger is wrapped around the outside of the disc and resting on the inside lip. Your middle finger should be completely straight, while your ring finger and pinky should be resting on the outside lip of the disc for support. With this type of grip, you have a wide-open shot at getting the maximum distance out of your disc.

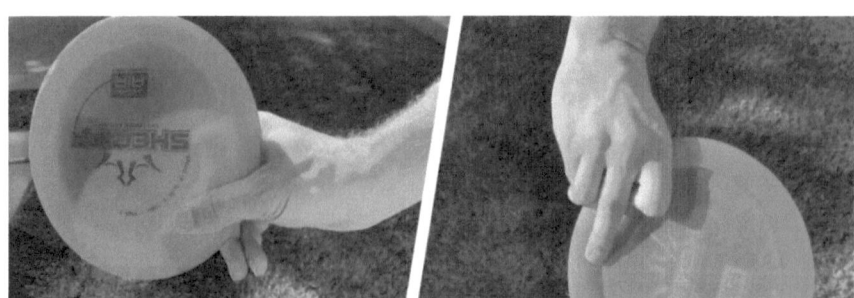

Extras

While the above-listed grips are the most common in disc golf, there are ways you can get more distance or accuracy from your grip. You can get more from your throw by altering your thumb position or grip pressure.

- **Thumb position**

The position of your thumb can help you change the forward angle of your disc. Altering your thumb position is particularly helpful when you often release the disc with the nose up. If the nose is up when you throw, it impacts the aerodynamics of the disc, thus reducing how far it travels. To correct this issue of your disc traveling with the nose up, position your thumb closer to the outside of the disc.

- **Grip pressure**

Also, how strongly you grip the disc can impact the control, spin, power, and flight distance. A firm grip lets you achieve this as opposed to a loose grip. Gripping the disc too much too can also negatively impact your throw. As you practice, aim to strike a balance on your grip pressure to get an optimal throw. A good rule of thumb is that if the disc wobbles leaving your hand, you need to increase how firmly you hold the disc.

How to Throw Disc Golf?

Throwing disc golf is pretty straightforward. You hold the disc in your dominant hand, reach back, pull through, and then release. However, if you want to increase your skills and throw more advanced shots, you need to learn a little bit more about the different types of throws in this game. In this book section, we will walk you through common throwing styles you can use in disc golf to improve your game.

- **Backhand**

The backhand is perhaps the most common throwing style in disc golf. It involves extending your throwing hands back towards the opposite side of your body and swinging it away/outwards from your body, releasing the disc as you throw. This throwing style mimics the motion you'd make when you pull or starting a lawn mower. As a beginner, the backhand throwing style is likely what you're learning.

- **Forehand**

The forehand throwing style is another common disc throwing style that is the opposite of the backhand throwing style. It spins in the opposite direction when you throw discs using this style. It involves extending your throwing arm back towards the side of your body and swinging it away from your body. This throwing style mimics someone skipping rocks on a pond.

- **Hyzer**

The hyzer is an angled disc throwing style where the disc's travel path turns to the thrower's left. This throwing style is perhaps the most basic angled throw in disc golf. The hyzer throwing style is handy in several throwing situations, such as obstacles in your path or a sharp dogleg left holes on the course.

- **Anhyzer**

The anhyzer throwing style is the opposite of the hyzer, where the disc angle of flight is towards the thrower's right. The anhyzer throwing style is great for throwing situations similar to the hyzer. You can use an anhyzer throwing style when an obstacle in your path or a sharp dogleg right hole.

- **Turnover shot**

The turnover shot is more of an advanced throwing style though it seems similar to the anhyzer throwing style. The turnover shot is ideal when throwing the disc to a dogleg right hole. Throwing with the turnover shot gives you a more deliberate shot. One thing you should note about this throwing style is that you are trying to get the disc to curve in the direction opposite to what it will naturally want to fade.

- **Roller shot**

You can think of the roller shot as an extreme turnover shot using a disc you are familiar with. When you use this throwing style, the disc should fall to the ground on its side and roll, hopefully slicing through obstacles you want to maneuver. The roller shot is a cool way to get your disc to cover more distance while maneuvering multiple obstacles.

- **S shot**

The S and roller shots are very similar as they involve great power and speed. So it's best to practice this shot, so it doesn't turn into a roller shot when you don't want a roller shot. The S shot starts flat and then gradually fades into a curve towards the end. It's best to use a disc with a decent speed (-2 to -3) and a low-speed fade (1 to 2).

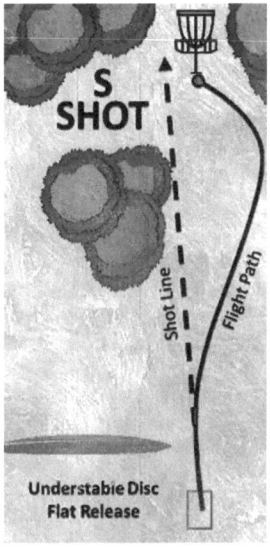

- **Hyzer flip**

Another disc golf throwing style you can add to your list to improve yourself is this hyzer flip. It is very similar to the S shot that involves throwing the disc on a hyzer angle, unlike the S shot that is thrown flat with no angle. When you throw a hyzer flip, the disc will start with the hyzer, turn over the other direction then fade back at the end.

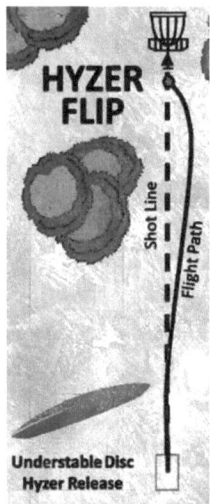

- **Flex shot**

The flex shot throwing style is one of the toughest you can learn in disc golf, but its benefits are tremendous for this type of throwing style. The flex shot follows a similar flight path as the S shot. For this throw, it is best to use an over stable disc with a decent amount of fade. As a beginner, it's helpful to practice the flex shot once you have developed some decent skill level.

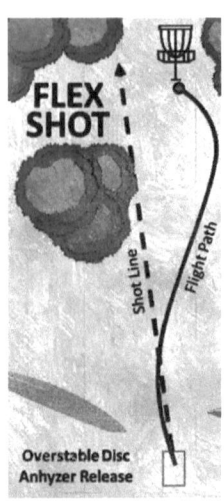

- **Thumber and Tomahawk shots**

With the thumber and tomahawk throwing style, the disc moves in a curve or corkscrew direction while in flight. Throwing the thumber and tomahawk shots curve in a particular way such that they essentially fly upside down at one point in their flight. To throw a thumber shot, hold the disc with your thumb on the inside of the disc. To throw a tomahawk shot, hold the disc with your thumb at the top of the disc and your middle and index finger on the inside of the ring.

THUMBER SHOT

TOMAHAWK SHOT

Guidelines to Play the Game

If you have noted everything so far, you should have already picked up on some of the guidelines for playing disc golf. While disc golf is a thorough game with its rules laid out by the PDGA, it is quite straightforward once you go through it. In this book section, we will break down the guidelines for playing disc golf into eight groups.

1. **Safety first**

    When playing disc golf, you must never throw your disc when other players are within range. Players are required to always give non-players the right of way. Also, it is important to always be aware of the surroundings and environment.

2. **Tee throws**

   Each throw begins with a tee throw. The tee throw must be completed behind or within the designated tee area. Exceeding the tee line will attract an extra throw penalty added to your cumulative throw.

3. **Throwing order**

   The throwing order is a guideline that determines who throws the next hole. The player with the least amount of throws on the previous hole will take the first tee on the next throw. After teeing off, the player whose disc is farthest from the hole will always throw first.

4. **Fairway throws**

   A fairway throw is a throw made from behind the lie. When the shot is within 10 meters of the target, the player is required not to move past the lie until the disc has come to a rest. A normal follow-through or run-up after release is allowed, provided the lie is within 10 meters of the target.

5. **Mandatory**

   A mandatory is one or more poles or trees the players must throw the disc pass as indicated by arrows. Failing to throw the disc past the mandatory will attract a penalty to re-throw from the previous lie from a designated drop zone area, which comes with a one-throw penalty.

6. **Unplayable lines**

    The unplayable lines are areas in the course that is above or below the ground. In such cases, the disc must be placed on the ground and thrown from lying on the ground.

7. **Out of bounds**

    In any designated out-of-bound area, if the disc should lie between a visible out-of-bound line (approximately 1 meter inbound from where the disc went out of bounds), the disc is considered out of bound.

8. **Completion of holes**

    A throw is considered completed if it comes to rest in the basket or chains of the hole.

Chapter 4
Equipment

Every sport is played with one or a couple of equipment. No matter what the guidelines govern the game, there is always a list of equipment used to play the game. And disc golf is no different, as it is played with a list of equipment. The most important equipment used in disc golf is the disc. However, there is other equipment used in the game.

In this chapter of this book, we will discuss everything equipment used in playing disc golf. Also, we will teach you how to choose the right disc for the game and how important a disc flight number is. So, stay with us as we go through this interesting journey together.

What Equipment is used to Play Disc Golf?

If you haven't noticed till now, disc golf is a type of sport that relies heavily on specific equipment to play. Unlike other sports where you can replace equipment and still have a great time playing, the disc golf is a very different version. In this section of this article, we will discuss the basic equipment you will need to play disc golf as a beginner.

- **Throwing Disc**

The throwing disc in disc golf is essential equipment in the game. It is a specialized disc round in shape and made of plastic or varying material. The throwing disc is what is thrown towards the basket in the game.

- **Carrying bag**

The carrying bag is another essential piece of equipment you will need to play the game. It is a regular bag in which you keep all your equipment. A simple backpack should suffice as a carrying bag.

- **Marker disc**

A marker disc is a smaller disc than a throwing disc. The marker disc is not thrown in the game. It is used to mark a player's lie on the course; when the marker disc is placed where the player's disc lies, the disc can then be picked up for the next throw.

- **Scorecard**

As you already know, disc golf is a competitive sport. Hence, it is important to keep track of each player's score. A scorecard comes in to conveniently help players in this aspect. With the scorecard, players can track their progress and their opponent's from round to round and set goals to achieve in other to win.

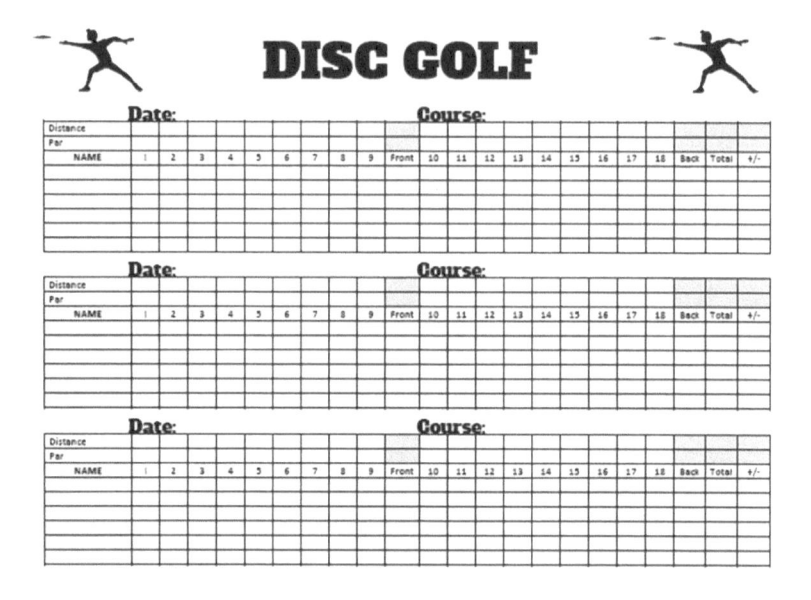

- **Tee signs**

Tee signs are equipment in disc golf used to map the course. Tee signs are important to improve the overall usability and player's experience. They provide important information such as out-of-bound areas, preferred flight paths, and distances and keep players on track and safe by pointing out hazards.

- **Basket**

Finally, the basket is another essential equipment used in the game. The basket is what players throw their disc at to make the disc land in it. The basket is made of chains assembled on a pole and a bowl in the middle.

What is Disc Golf made of?

Disc golf discs are made of a plastic material. Specialized plastic material like polypropylene plastic, also known as polypropene, is what most manufacturers use. There are several polymers of this resin, such as a thermoplastic elastomer, polyethylene, and polyurethane, to mention a few. Hence, a wide variety of discs can be made with this plastic.

The reason manufacturers choose to use polypropene is because they are durable yet lightweight, making the discs travel the expected distance. The production process of disc golf discs is fairly complex, but basically, the plastic is injected into molds and refrigerated until it hardens.

How to Choose the Right Disc?

There is several disc golf manufacturers, meaning there are too many discs to count. Choosing the right one from the massive pile of discs can be difficult if you don't know what to look for. Consider the following features of discs below to filter through the several discs in the market so you can choose the right disc.

- **The material used in making the disc**

    While plastic is a widely accepted material for making the disc, the basic plastic to the more expensive premium plastic can affect stability and flight distance. Before getting any disc golf, ensure it is made of plastic that best suits your playing style.

- **Disc weight**

    As a beginner, you want to aim for a lighters disc. The weight of the disc you choose can impact your play in many ways. This is because lighter discs are much easier to throw as they are more under stable. In comparison, heavier disc tends to be more over stable. We will talk more about this later in this chapter.

- **Disc flight number**

    Every disc used in disc golf falls under a flight number. This flight number determines how the disc will travel. It's important to consider the disc flight number before buying one. We will talk more about this later in this chapter.

- **Color**

    When buying discs for disc golf, aim for one with a brighter color. While the color does not impact your throw, it does make it easy to find your disc. However, you don't need to worry much about the color of the disc you use for approach or as putters as they usually travel a far distance, hence hardly get lost.

Understanding Disc Flight Number?

One thing you may have noticed on disc golf is a series of four or five numbers printed on it. These numbers are the flight number, and they give you an idea of the disc's flight path even before it is thrown. It is important to take note of the disc flight number before buying one. The numbers you see on a disc flight number can be categorized into the following:

- **Speed**

    The speed flight rating is the first number on the disc and can be labeled between 1 and 14. You can think of the speed flight rating as the amount of power that is behind the disc. The lower the speed rating, the easier it will be to throw; however, they wouldn't travel far. If you are looking for a disc that travels more distance, aim for a disc with a higher speed rating. However, the higher the speed rating, the harder it will be to throw the disc.

- **Glide**

   Next to the speed rating is the gliding rating, which can be labeled between 1 and 7. The glide rating indicates the disc's ability to stay in the air and flies towards the basket. You should aim for a disc with a low glide rating for a putter disc, as there is a limited landing area for this throw. A disc with a low glide rating tends to rely more on the power you put when throwing it to cover more area, whereas a disc with a high gliding rating travels more distance.

- **Turn**

   Next to the gliding rating is the turn rating which can be labeled between +1 and -5. The turn flight rating can be used to describe the high-speed stability of a disc. When you throw a disc, its speed starts to build, and it will want to start turning. The closer to the positive side of the turn rating of a disc, the more resistant it is to turn at high speed. Most beginners use a disc with a negative turn rating because they cannot get it up to speed.

- **Fade**

   On disc golf discs, the fourth flight rating is the fade flight rating which is usually the last number you see on the disc. But on discs with five flight ratings, the fade is the second to the last and can be labeled between 0 and 5. The fade rating describes the end of the disc's flight. Fade can also be used to

Equipment

describe the stability of the disc at low speed. When a disc begins to lose power during flight, the fade begins. A disc with a higher fade rating tends to start its fade earlier than a disc with a lower fade rating.

- **Stable**

The stable flight rating is not a rating you see on all discs. But if a flight disc happens to have it, it is often written last and can be labeled between -3 and 3. The stable flight rating tells you how stable the disc is when you throw it. The higher the stable flight rating, the more stable the disc will be, while the lower the stable flight rating, the less stable it will be.

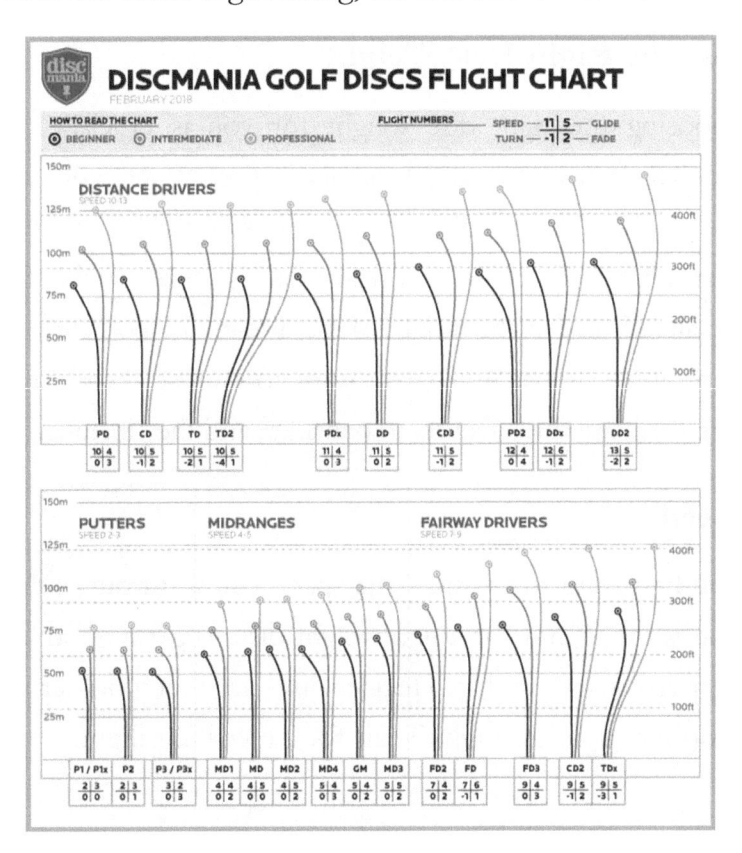

Beginner Disc Golf Weight

Disc golf discs come in varying weights as well. They are measured in grams and can be found on the body of the disc. As a beginner, it is ideal to go for a lighter disc, and as you advance, you can try a heavier one. A lightweight disc is ideal for beginners because most beginners struggle with getting the heavier disc up to speed or traveling a long distance. Lightweight discs are easier to get up to speed and travel a long distance. Hence, it is ideal to go for a disc around 170 grams. And as you advance, you can use a disc as heavy as 180 grams. Keep reading to learn how to choose the right disc weight for you.

Choose the Right Disc Weight

Choosing the right disc weight for you is crucial as it can significantly impact the flight of your disc. When you want to choose a disc that is right for you, it is important to consider whether a lightweight disc or a heavy disc is more suitable for you. As you already know, the weight of the disc in disc golf varies to suit different applications. When you want to choose the right weight for you, there are three factors to consider, and they include:

- **Speed**

    You first want to consider the speed you want out of the disc. You want to aim for a lightweight disc to get a good amount of speed from the disc. Heavier discs are much harder to get a good nice spin through the air for a nice long flight.

- **Distance**

    Another thing you should consider when choosing a disc is the distance you want it to travel. A lighter disc tends to travel farther than a heavier disc. Lighter disc travels farther because they are easier to throw with more velocity than heavier discs.

- **Ease to throw**

    Generally, because lighter discs weigh less, they are easier to throw. Players require less effort to throw it than heavier discs. For example, throwing a light disc makes sense when throwing uphill to get more distance. Light discs will also make a perfect disc for tailwind drives.

- **Accuracy**

    Also, lighter discs have higher accuracy than heavier discs. However, they can easily be affected by winds. But because lighter discs do not require much effort, players can throw them with more precision. Hence, getting a lighter disc as a putter or for an approach is important.

Best Stores to Buy Disc Golf Equipment

When you want to buy your first disc golf, there are a few places we can recommend you check for the cheapest and best of products. While the places to buy disc golf equipment are not limited to these stores, they are the most recommended from our personal experience. When shopping for disc golf equipment, check out the following stores:

- **Amazon**

    Amazon is American multinational e-commerce that has been in the industry since 1994. With decades of experience in the industry, they have become a giant in the industry. When it comes to buying disc golf equipment, we recommend this platform as it gives you the luxury of finding the cheapest disc golf equipment you need from a long list of sellers who will ship it to your doorstep.

- **Disc Golf Company**

    The most reliable place to shop for disc golf equipment is from Disc Golf Company. Buying directly from the company is cheaper. However, some companies may require you to buy in a larger quantity. If you want to buy directly from a disc golf company, look for on-sale offers. With an on-sale offer, you can buy several disc golf equipment at a discount.

- **eBay**

    eBay is a marketplace like Amazon, founded in 1995. But unlike Amazon, eBay's online marketplace connects consumers to buy and sell used items on the platform. With eBay, you can buy a fairly used item that suits your buying needs at a discount.

- **Local store**

    Finally, you don't need to buy a disc from an online platform. There are several local stores you can walk into to pick out a disc that is right for you. At a local store like Walmart and so on, you can easily shop for a disc to buy. The advantage of buying a disc at a local store is that you can have a hand feel of what you are buying to ensure it is right for you.

Build Your Own Disc Golf Bag

With everything said about the equipment used to play disc golf, let's discuss how to build your bag. Every player's need is different. Hence, what I may need to enjoy my play time may be very different from what another player will need. In other words, there are a couple of things you can keep an eye on. When building a disc golf bag, consider the things you need and keep them in your bag. Remember you need more than one disc to make taking different types of shots easier. Whether you are taking three discs in your bag or thirty discs, ensure each one has a special function they serve. For example, you want to get a disc or some discs as distance driver, some as fairway driver, some as midrange, and some as putt approach.

Miscellaneous Items in Your Bag

Aside from carrying the disc, there are other miscellaneous items you bring to the game. These items are meant to make your game play fun. Below is a list of items that you can stuff in a bag.

- **Snacks**

    It is always a good idea to have a snack in your bag when playing disc golf. The snack doesn't necessarily need to be anything too special. It has fulfilled its purpose as long as it keeps your body energized. A protein or energy bar is a great example of a snack in your bag.

- **Water bottle**

    Additionally, you should always have a bottle of water in your bag. The water bottle will ensure you stay hydrated, as when the game starts, you wouldn't be able to go out of the playing zone in seek of water. So, it's best to have it handy in your bag in case you get thirsty from all the activities in the game.

- **Shoe**

    Of course, you weren't planning to be barefooted when playing disc golf. Hence, getting a nice pair of sneakers and keeping them in your bag is essential. This is important so that you have everything you need whenever you are heading out for a nice game with family or friends.

- **Towel**

    A towel is another helpful piece you can throw in your bag. They come in handy when you or your disc becomes wet or muddy. Also, expect to get sweaty playing the game. So, a towel will go a long way if you have it in your bag.

- **Disc golf removal**

    A disc golf removal also comes in handy when picking up your disc from far to reach location. For example, when the disc lands on a tree or in a pond, a disc golf removal saves you the hassle of losing your disc. With disc golf removable, you can retrieve your disc from the water, a tall tree, or anywhere else without using your hands.

Chapter 5
How to Play the Game?

If you have been following through with us from chapter 1 up to this chapter, we would love to first congratulate you on your steady progress so far. In this chapter, we will expound a little more on how to play the game. Playing disc golf is fairly straightforward. However, if you want to stand out, it is essential to understand some of the playing strategies. Hence, this chapter will teach us how to generate the correct spin and speed and be a good putter overall. So, let's get started.

All You Need to Get Started

We have talked about the fact that there are different discs you can buy. We also discussed the flight rating system and how to use it. Now we will be using that knowledge in this section to recommend the types of disc you need for certain throws. As a beginner, there are three main approaches to landing a disc into the basket you should have at the back of your mind. They include the driver throw, the mid-range throw, and the putter throw. With a good understanding of the disc to use in these three throws, you shouldn't have any issue landing the disc in the basket.

As a beginner, you need a specialized disc for a driver throw, as what you want here is a disc that travels the farthest distance. For this, we recommend you get four to six different discs with a flight rating within the range of 7-13/4-5/(-3)-0/1-3. For the midrange throw, you want a disc with a high control level. For this, we recommend getting three or more discs with a flight rating within the range of 4-5/4-5/ (-1)-(-3)/0-1. And finally, the putter throw should be done with a disc that has a slow-flying, deep rimmed and accurate throw over a short distance. We recommend getting up to six discs for this with a flight rating within the range of 2-4/3-4/0-(-2)/0-3.

Generating the Correct Turn and Speed

Another thing you need to help you advance your play in disc golf is being able to generate the correct spin and speed. While we have spoken about speed in previous chapters, we will teach you how to get the right speed in this chapter. We will be dividing this section into two parts, one teaching you how to get the correct spin while the other teaching you how to get the correct speed.

How to generate the correct turn?

One of the flight characteristics is the disc turn when you throw a disc. Ideally, the disc is meant to turn during the fastest part of its flight. But how much to the right it turns depends on the type of disc you use and your arm strength. The degree of turn on a disc is the third flight rating in the flight rating system we discussed in previous chapters and can range from -5 to +1. Different discs have different degrees of resistance to high-speed turns. The more resistant a disc is to spin, the more stable it is.

The closer a disc rating is to the -5 mark, the more turn the disc will have. These discs are classified as understable. Discs with a moderate amount of turn are stable, and discs that resist turning right even at high speed are overstable. Many beginners struggle with getting the disc to turn appropriately. For this reason, it is best to avoid an overstable disc and aim for an understable one. Also, a disc with less fade will go a long way in helping you achieve that perfect turn. You should also work on your throw to get it fasters. The anhyzer throw is recommended. And ensure you go for a lot of practice to generate the correct turn.

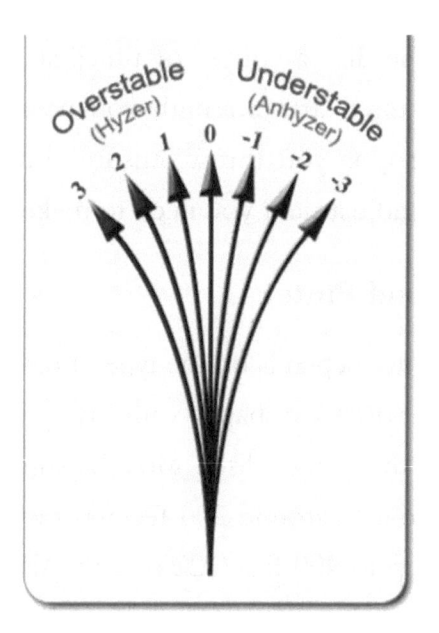

How to generate the correct speed?

The trick to generating the correct speed comes down to two factors, the disc you are using and your arm power. Different discs come with different speed flight ratings. So, generating the correct speed is what works best for the disc. The maximum speed a disc can travel is 14. But buying and throwing a 14 disc does not make you better than someone throwing a 12 disc. Matching the disc with the correct arm speed matters a lot. Some of the best players in the world don't even throw a 14 disc. For example, World Champion Gregg Barsby throws a 7 speed disc for his primary driver.

If you don't throw at the right speed, the disc will lift and finish hard to the left without gaining much distance. Similarly, if you throw faster than the speed of the disc, it creates a little wobble in the flight. Generating the correct speed takes a lot of practice. Throw the disc a couple of times at varying speeds to determine the required arm strength you need to get it to the correct speed. Also, as you throw, ensure you watch the flight path and see what adjustment you need to make.

How to be a Good Putter

Throwing a putter depends on the type of disc you use and how you throw it. Putter discs are shaped with a deep rim, fly slowly, and are more accurate than other discs. Most beginners throw a putter for shots maxing out at around 200 feet/60 meters, but advanced players can get it up to 400 feet/122 meters. Also, when shopping for a putter disc, note that its speed range between 1 and 4. Its other three flight numbers are spread all over the place with understable putters with higher turn numbers, overstable putters with a high fade number, and putters with superior glide.

When you want to throw a putter disc, a fan grip helps. The fan grip is held by spreading your middle, ring, and pinky finger over the underside of the disc and your thumb sitting on top of the disc. Your pointer finger should be on the rim, and for throwing, your pointer finger should be tucked inside the rim slightly. Don't long run when you want to throw a putter. Rather a standstill throw with controlled throwing motion will maximize success. Also, when throwing a putter, throw at 40 to 50 percent power and focus more on throwing the disc flat.

How to Throw a Mid-Range Disc

Mid-range discs are that category of discs that any player can control. Mid-range discs fall perfectly between putters and driver discs. And in most players' bags, there is usually a staple of mid-range discs in it. Mid-range discs have a speed flight rating ranging from 2 to 6, although most discs fall between speeds 4 and 6. And when thrown properly, a mid-range disc has a flight distance of 300 feet/91.5 meters. However, some advanced players can get a mid-range disc up to 450 feet/137 meters.

The fan grip can also give you enough power to get it in the right flight path when throwing a mid-range disc. However, the difference between gripping a putter disc and a mid-range disc is how you position your index finger. You want to tuck your index finger slightly into and underneath the rim with a midrange disc. And if your grip is correct, you should use about 60-70 percent of power to throw and focus on a flat release out of hand.

How to Throw a Driver Disc

Throwing a driver disc is all about getting the disc to travel the farthest distance possible. A typical driver's disc can travel a distance of over 600 feet/183 meters. Even when the conditions are normal, a putter or mid-range disc cannot go the distance a driver disc can. The driver disc can travel so far because of its wide, shallow, sharp rim and flat aerodynamic shapes. Do not use a driver disc for a throw less than 300 feet/91 meters. Also, a typical driver disc has a speed flight rating between 9 and 15.

When thrown correctly, a driver disc mimics a disc with a slower flight rating, ranging all over instability. Although when a driver disc is underthrown, it becomes overstable and fades out faster. To correctly throw a driver disc, it is recommended to use a power grip, as you want to get as much power in your throw as possible. For a power grip, place your thumb on the top side of the disc and your index, middle, ring, and pinky finger stacked together and wrapped tightly inside the rim.

Chapter 6
Some More Pointers Before You Start Playing

You are equipped with everything basic to start playing disc golf at this stage. However, before heading out to the fields for your first real game, we recommend considering some more pointers to get started. We wouldn't crack your brains in this chapter with complicated terminologies or mathematical calculations. Rather we will be talking about some of the basic things that will help you play more comfortably without beating around the bush.

Choose a Beginner-Friendly Course

Even though at this stage you already understand the playing technique of the game, not all courses are ideal for you as a beginner. A disc golf course varies in challenges. Hence, as a beginner, it is recommended that you go for an easier course; as you advance, you can start attempting more challenging courses. Disc golf courses can be classified based on the challenges they offer and how well equipped they are so that when searching, you can tell which course is ideal for your level. The course is classed using the letters AAA-A, BB-B, C, and D. Courses with an AAA rating indicate a full-length competition level and are very difficult. In comparison, courses with a D rating are short and more beginner-friendly. The table below should explain better.

Classification	AAA	AA	A	BB	B	C	D
Amount of holes	18+	18+	18+	9-17	9-17	7-17	6 or less
Avg hole length (ft)	450+	330-450	<330	330+	245-330	<245	Not specified
Avg hole length (m)	140+	100-140	<100	100+	75-100	<75	Not specified
Par	64+	58+	Not specified	At least one par 4	Not specified	Not specified	Not specified

While searching for an ideal beginner-friendly course for yourself, you must consider the following features:

- **Location**

   Where you live can influence whether or not you will find a suitable disc golf course. If you find it hard to locate an ideal location with a level ideal for you, we recommend using any online location resources (there are several). You can also download the Professional Disc Golf Association mobile app (UDisc app) to find several helpful information on where to go to play disc golf at your level.

   Creating a simple disc golf course isn't hard. All you need is a field, a basket, and your disc. What you may find challenging is sourcing space to set it up. If you can have that settled, then you are good to go. But in a case where the location you live, have no disc golf course at a level recommended for you, and then it would make sense to create one for yourself.

- **Number of holes**

   Another feature to consider when searching for that ideal disc golf is the number of holes on the course. There are disc golf courses with as many as 20 holes and those with less than 6 holes. As a beginner, you want to aim for a course with the fewest holes. Where there are more holes in the course, automatically, the course tends to be designed as more challenging.

While it is good to face challenges to grow, at the same time, when the challenges are too challenging, it can deter your progress and even frustrate you to give up on the game. For this reason, we often recommend players play in a course with the fewest number of holes. This way, they can easily get the disc in the hole and complete the course in no time. The feeling of accomplishing or reaching a goal is encouraging. It will help you want to try harder in more challenging courses.

- **Average hole length**

It is also important to consider the layout of the course. This includes considering the foot range of the course. As a beginner, it is recommended to go for a course that is only a few feet or meters long. The longer the course, the more challenging it will be for a beginner. Since as a beginner, you are yet to fully develop your arm strength and get the disc to travel far distance or even to get the disc turning right.

Starting with a short disc golf course will encourage you as you will see results from your placing session. A disc golf course about 100 to 250 feet long is ideal for beginners. As a beginner, you can also aim to play at a pitch or putt golf course as they will help you learn more about the basics and have fun.

Dress Appropriately

There is an acceptable dress to wear and an unacceptable way to dress when going to play disc golf. It goes without saying that when playing disc golf, it is important to wear something very comfortable. However, it is still vital that you abide by the dressing code of the game. While in an informal setting, how you dress doesn't concern anyone, but it is a good practice to abide by the proper dressing code in any setting.

If anyone were to violate the dressing code of the game, such a person would violate courtesy and be penalized. Also, one thing you should know about dressing appropriately for disc golf is that everyone, both competitors and staff, must wear a shirt. Also, competitors and staff are required to wear proper shoes as players are not allowed to wear sandals or slides. Below is a list of things to note when dressing for a disc golf game:

- Players and staff must maintain a clean and well-groomed appearance at all events.

- Players must wear a shirt covering the upper chest area with a well-tailored collar and sleeves covering the upper arms. Although women can wear sleeveless shirts with collars, tank tops are not allowed.

- Tee shirts are not allowed except for competitors, juniors, and beginners in preliminary rounds.

- Shits hanging down lower than the bottom hemline must be tucked in.

- No ripped shorts, shirt, and pants are allowed on the course

- No offensive, obscene, profane logos and slogans are allowed on any clothing.

- Players and staff must abide by the dress code of the game from the start to the finish of each event.

- Players who don't make the cut but wish to speculate are not required to abide by the dress code of the game.

Prepping Yourself before Playing

Whether this is your first game or your hundredth, it is always a good idea to prep yourself before the play. Feeling anxiety, nervousness, or even confidence moments before the game is normal. However, what you do during this period can either make or break your performance during the event. We often advise beginners to channel whatever energy they are feeling into their play and be physically and mentally prepared for the game. Here are a few tips on how to prepare yourself before the play:

- **Scout the course**

    Before the game starts, you can take the time to scout the course and, if possible, take a walk around the course to understand the layout of the land. Take note of the distance to the baskets and where the first shot will be taken. If it is a course you aren't familiar with, it will help to practice it a day before the game day just to familiarize yourself with it.

- **Develop a playing strategy**

    After scouting the course a good number of times and taking note of some key things about the layout, develop a workable playing strategy. Pick out the best discs you will use at each stage. Select a disc you will use at each point on the course. For example, select a disc you will use for the drive, the one you will use to approach, and one for putting.

- **Practice**

    Practicing before playing a match cannot be substituted for anything else. When you practice, you familiarize yourself with the course so that it becomes easy to put the disc in the basket. With muscle memory also kicking in, you shouldn't have any issues during the actual game.

- **Get your bag ready**

    Lastly, when it's almost time for the game, ensure your bag is properly packed with everything you need. Reconfirm the discs in your bag, ensuring you have the right discs with the right flight rating for the game. Add every other miscellaneous item you might need during the game so you don't get stranded.

Check the Surface

Disc golf is one of those few sports that are not played on a standardized playing surface. You can theoretically play the game anywhere if you have a hole, a club, and teeing ground. However, it is important to take your time to check what the surface of the course looks like. Generally, the tee area where the game starts is often flat and provides a good distance if you want to follow up your throw with a run-up.

The rest of the course may not be as flat as you want and may also contain water ponds and other obstacles. Take note of these obstacles so that you avoid them when throwing your discs. Landing on a tree or in a pond of water may affect your score as you may be penalized with an extra throw. Moreover, throwing from the bottom of a tree or a pond of water may not be the best experience.

Chapter 7
Physical Fitness and Safety Measures

When you play disc golf regularly, though the sport is fun and exciting, at the same time, you are also going to enjoy diverse physical fitness benefits. Over the past few years, there have been several reports about people who play disc golf frequently and noticed a significant improvement in their overall health. In this chapter, we will discuss some of the physical fitness benefits you stand to gain when playing disc golf. Disc golf also has mental benefits, but we will leave that for another chapter.

Physical Fitness Benefits of Playing Disc Golf

Consistently playing disc golf has several physical benefits. If you are curious about what physical fitness benefits you stand to gain when playing disc golf, then you are in the right place. Here are seven physical fitness benefits you stand to gain from playing disc golf:

- **Excellent full-body exercise**

  Disc golf is a type of game that involves the movement of almost every part of your body. The running, stretching of your arms and everything constitutes a variety of exercises in one activity. So, by playing disc golf, you are generally working out your whole body. Generally, playing the whole a standard disc golf course can be equivalent to walking miles. So, when you play this game, you will be strengthening your lower and upper body muscles. In addition, throwing the disc involves exercising your chest, triceps, back, and shoulders.

- **Energy booster**

Another physical benefit of playing disc golf is that it can be a real energy booster for those with several medical conditions. Contrary to what you may have thought, playing disc golf regularly can reduce the feeling of fatigue. Playing disc golf can also significantly benefit people with chronic fatigue syndrome and other health conditions. One can even take disc golf as a form of passive therapy to boost stretching and relaxation as a whole.

- **Improves heart health**

Many people underestimate the importance of their heart health. And in reality, you will be surprised at how much your lifestyle can affect your heart health. For example, when you are not eating healthy, this can cause the buildup of trans fatty acids in your body, which can clog the free flow of blood in and out of the heart, thus causing elevated blood pressure and other complication with the heart. However, the good news is that physical activity such as playing disc golf can help break down trans fatty acid faster than when you do nothing.

- **Helps manage weight**

Inactivity is the major cause of weight gain and obesity. If you aim to manage your body weight, playing disc golf is an excellent way to go about it. Playing disc golf, a form of physical activity, helps you manage your weight in three ways. Firstly, when you play disc golf, it causes food to digest faster. Secondly, playing disc golf helps manage bodily functions such as heartbeat and breathing, which can increase or decrease your appetite. Lastly, when you play disc golf, aerobic exercise such as playing disc golf will help maximize fat loss and mass muscle maintenance, which is essential in keeping the weight off and lean muscle mass.

- **Good for bones and muscles**

    While disc golf may not be the most intense physical activity, it goes a long way in improving bone density and maintaining muscle strength. Because disc golf involves the movement of several parts of your body and joints, which promotes the muscle's absorption of amino acids, this helps release hormones that promote the growth of bones and muscles.

- **Makes the skin healthier**

    Going out of your home to play disc golf is a better activity than staying indoors all day long. Exposure to a decent amount of sunlight will aid in producing vitamin D, which is essential in making the skin healthier. Also, performing physical activities such as playing golf can help you sweat, which will eliminate free radicals that can cause oxidative stress to the skin.

- **Manage chronic diseases**

    People dealing with chronic diseases can use disc golf to manage it and perform physical activity. Consistently playing disc golf can help improve heart health, insulin sensitivity, and overall body composition. Disc golf can also be used to decrease cholesterol and blood pressure levels greatly, making it a very useful activity. And best of all, the sport is relatively fun to play and does not require much strength to play.

Safety Measure to Observe in Disc Golf

Now that you know some of the physical health benefits of playing disc golf let's look at some of the safety measures you are to observe when playing the game. When engaging in physical activity such as playing disc golf, there is always the risk of an injury occurring. Player might experience back pain, muscle strain, injuries, tissue injury, etc. Below are some of the safety measures put in place that players should observe to avoid an accident:

- Players must throw the disc from designated areas for challenge and safety reasons.

- Players are to ensure the fairway is clear before throwing the disc.

- The disc is not to be thrown at trees, lamps, and so on, as this can attract a penalty of an extra throw.

- Disc golf courses are only opened during daylight hours

- All fenced and roadways areas are out of bounds.

Chapter 8
Tack Your Score

What is the point of a disc golf game if there is no winner at the end? Players can determine who is winning or losing in the game by tacking their score. Keeping a record of scores in the game is fairly straightforward. The trick is to know what counts as a valid throw and what can cause you to be penalized. Once you are familiar with the sport's rules, as explained in previous chapters, you can tack your score yourself. In this chapter, we will teach you how to tack your score, so you know if you are ahead or behind in the sport.

Challenge Your Memory – Remember the Scores

While disc golf is a different game, you will still come across many terms used in golf. If you are unfamiliar with the terms in golf, then you wouldn't understand what they mean in disc golf. So you can accurately score yourself, we recommend you challenge your memory to understand the following terms:

- **Ace**

When playing disc golf, you want to aim to score an ace. An ace is a term used to describe a situation when you can achieve a hole in one throw. While this type of throw is very difficult on some disc golf courses, it is possible to make such a throw-in several courses.

- **Par**

    Par is a term used in disc golf to describe how many throws you can take per hole to put the disc in the basket without penalties. If you go over par, it tends to hurt your score, so be careful when throwing.

- **Birdie**

    Technically, birdie is a term used under par in disc golf. You've got a birdie when a player manages the number of throws under par and can get the disc into the hole with an extra throw to go. Having a birdie will contribute positively to your score, so taking those throws with care is helpful.

- **Eagle**

    Sometimes, you may do better in a disc golf session than in a birdie. If you can have two extra throws left in your par, you have scored an eagle. Having an eagle earns you even better scores, so it helps to get enough food at the game to get the disc in the basket with the fewest throws possible.

- **Bogey**

    Of course, we shouldn't expect everyone to play at their best every single time, and that is alright. If you are not having a great day and surpassing par by one, then you have yourself a bogey. Getting a bogey wouldn't help your score, but it will not drag you down too far. Just ensure you don't make getting bogeys a habit.

- **Double Bogie**

    If you missed paying by two, you have scored a double bogie. Getting a score does not help favor your score down the line. So try as much as you can to avoid getting a double bogie. Players can also get a triple bogie and higher depending on how many throws away they missed par.

- **Extra Throw**

    And if you are having an extremely bad day, then you might get an extra throw on your score. Extra throws are added to your score when you accidentally throw the disc into water or out of bound. You should try to attain an extra throw as it is not good for your score.

Mark Your Score on a Paper Score Card

Now that you know a few things about scoring yourself let's take things a notch higher. Based on the information so far, this section will discuss how to mark your score in disc golf. There are several ways you can go about marking your score. The first thing you need to get is a paper scorecard. There are sources you can get a PDF copy of it, which you can print out for use to keep track of your score. With several places to get a scorecard, you should find it difficult to get your hands on a standard one. But for this section's sake, we will use a paper score card.

The scorecard used in disc golf essentially has a slot where you can indicate the distance of the course, the par, the player's name, front, back, and total. Let's say, for example, if you are throwing on a par with 4 holes, you have four throws to sink the disc in the basket. So, when you take your first throw off the tee, the second throw should take the disc closer to the basket, and it is possible to sink it in the basket. If the disc does not sink in the basket, you can try to sink it with the third or the fourth. Each throw you make to put the disc in the hole makes up your total score. Getting the basket in the hole with the least number of throws will give you a better score.

Use Your Smartphone

If using the paper and pencil scoring method seems like a lot of work, you can use your smartphone. There are several mobile apps you can download that will help you keep track of your progress in the game. Apps like the Professional Disc Golf Association App, UDisc Disc Golf App, and so on are examples of apps available on iOS and Androids that helps you intelligently keep track of your score in the game. These apps also have additional features that help you advance your disc-playing journey. So if you are a beginner, it helps to take advantage of these apps to get the most out of the sport.

July Play for Fun

If you are looking forward to your first disc golf tournament, then July is the month on your calendar you should mark. Several tournaments in disc golf are often played during July, making it the perfect time to keep an eye out for your favorite tournament to compete in. Look out for tournaments that will hold in your area or neighboring towns, and make it a date to have fun playing the course. With a little bit of luck and improved playing skills, you might just take home the winning prize and a medal to your name.

Chapter 9
Mental Well-Being

What aspect are we talking about when we say playing disc golf can help improve a player's mental well-being? While not many people consider this, playing disc golf can greatly impact the player's mental well-being. Having solid mental well-being helps you cope better with the stress of life and realize your abilities. You can also learn better and work more productively with solid mental well-being. In this chapter, we will discuss ten ways playing disc golf can improve a player's mental well-being.

1. **Mood boost**

    If you are feeling sad, playing disc golf can significantly improve your mood even before you get midway into the game. Disc golf can boost players' mood because it helps improve the secretion of a hormone in the brain known as serotine. Serotine plays a vital role in the brain, such as balancing mood, sleep, desires, etc.

2. **Reduces stress**

    Playing disc golf is another great way to relieve stress. Many people often think that while playing disc golf, there isn't much walking around or real exercise, but this isn't true. Disc golf involves a decent amount of exercise that is enough to keep anyone's stress level to a minimum. After a few minutes into the game, you will start noticing your heart beating faster and more oxygen flowing into the brain. This process is not only stress-relieving but also helps you think more clearly, which improves your memory. Overall, disc golf is a great activity that strengthens the heart as well as the brain.

3. **Keeps anxiety level to a minimal**

    Suppose you are the type of person that easily feels anxious about everything. Or, if you are someone that over thinks every little chance, then disc golf is a type of sport that can help keep your anxiety level to a minimum. Playing a game like disc golf keeps your mind preoccupied, leaving no chance to over think. Moreover, you will be interacting with other people, which will help you learn new things. All you need to do is find the nearest disc golf course and start playing to get your mind off the stresses of life.

4. **Improves sleep quality**

    After a nice, fun time playing disc golf, all you would feel like doing is having a nice rest. If you were to be home or indoors all day long, the probability you will have a good rest is slim. But after playing disc golf, you would have exercised the body, sweat a little, and even exercised the brain. Hence, when you crash on your bed, all that will be on your mind is to get some rest.

5. **Promotes self-confidence**

    Do you lack self-confidence? If you do, playing a game like disc golf helps you overcome this anxiety. Self-confidence is a trait that helps anyone stand out, even in a large crowd. Lacking it can affect a person in so many areas of their life that you can't begin to phantom. If anyone is finding it difficult to have self-confidence, playing disc golf helps such a person face their challenge head-on. Disc golf is a public game; hence, there will be spectators, and players will be the center of attraction. Hence, if anyone can handle such attention, such person has improved their self-confidence.

6. **Improves social life**

    Playing disc golf is a great way to improve your social life. You will interact with others when you go out to play disc golf. There will always be one or two things you might want to ask someone or someone will want to ask you. From there, one thing will lead to another that will always spark a conversation. Hence, you will no doubt have a better social life by simply taking yourself to a gathering like playing disc golf. And who knows, you might be able to make some real and long-term friends.

7. **Provides a sense of achievement**

    Playing disc golf can also help fill up a void in you. The feeling of succeeding at something, no matter what it is, can provide you with a sense of achievement. For example, successfully throwing a disc into the basket can bring you much joy. And the best part about playing disc golf is that it does not compulsorily mean you have to be the winner of the game to have this feeling of achievement. Although becoming the game's winner does help give you a great feeling.

8. **Build independence**

    If you are trying to build a sense of independence, then playing disc golf can help you achieve that. Disc golf is that type of game that each player plays for themselves. Hence, the only person you can rely on in the game to win is yourself. If you play the game well, it will reflect on your result. And the truth is that if you play the game well, it will boost your confidence and how much confidence you have in your ability as an individual.

9. **Develop patience**

    Playing disc golf can also serve as a means to develop your patience. Patience is a virtue that can help you in several aspects of your life. The diverse challenges in a disc golf course can be quite challenging. Being able to continuously play disc golf and handle the challenges of the course will help you a great deal in developing an attitude of patience. To be able to master the game takes time and patience. Hence, patience is a course that is often learned from playing disc golf.

10. **Helps players understand their body**

    Disc golf also helps players become aware of their body alignment and position. When players want to take a shot in disc golf, they must understand their body as it helps them get the best shot. This requirement can ground individuals who tend to drift mentally. In addition to this, playing disc golf can help players know their limits and things their body can comfortably handle, and those things it can't handle

Chapter 10
Tips and Tricks of the Game for Beginners

We commend you for reading this book to its final chapter, as it has not been an easy journey so far. At this point, you already have all you need to head to the field to play disc golf. It is expected that you shouldn't find it difficult to perform certain basic tasks in the games. For example, you shouldn't find it difficult holding a disc or taking a shot.

While we undoubtedly believe in your playing skills at this point, we would like to share a few tips and tricks that you can use to improve yourself even further. Think of it more like in this chapter; we will share ways you can take what you've learnt higher.

Proper Technique to Throw a Disc

Anyone can throw a disc in disc golf. But not anyone can throw it properly. While we expect you to already know how to throw, we will be sharing with you seven throwing technique tips to help you properly throw a disc every time. In other words, proper technique matters because when you learn the fundamentals of the game, all other parts will improve.

- **Your grip is important.**

    The importance of having a good grip cannot be overemphasized enough. And when we say good grip, we do not mean holding the disc with so much strength. Rather, your grip has to be such that it's not too tight or too loose. If you hold the disc too tight, you will leave it late, thus sending it in the wrong direction. Similarly, if you hold the disc too loose, it could slip, sending it in the wrong direction.

- **Use a good hip rotation.**

    Another thing you can do to properly throw a disc is to rotate your hip while throwing. A good hip rotation while you throw helps maintain balance yet gives you enough power to throw a required distance. And when you lower yourself by bending your knee to the ground, you can balance yourself even more.

- **The back reach**

    The back reach is extremely simple as it involves reaching back diagonally at about a 45-degree angle towards the ground and your back leg. Adding more hip rotation before the throw helps you achieve more back reach. It also helps to fully extend your arm to maximize your throw. And the more back reaches you can get, the more momentum, power, and velocity you get on the throw.

- **Look away from your line of sight.**

    While you go for the back reach to throw, it may seem only logical to keep your eyes on the target, don't. Instead, what you want to do in this situation is to look down and away from the disc. Doing this will help you maximize your hip rotation, giving you more power and velocity to achieve more overall distance. And once you come back from the back reach, you will lock back onto the target.

- **Lead with your elbow**

    Once you come out of the back reach, then you can proceed with the throwing motion. For this, it is crucial how you come out to throw. When turning around to throw, you want to ensure you lead the throw with your elbow. The next motion needs to be more of a straight light through the throw rather than a circular motion. And while you are at it, keep the disc close to your chest.

- **Use a big, strong final step.**

    You should already know not to run up on the tee pad to get momentum by now. The trick to getting momentum is to take a big and strong step at the end of the drive. Taking a big step at the end is not very hard since your body's momentum is carrying you towards that step. Once you take that step, use your back leg to push off as hard as possible to get an extra couple of feet on top of the throw. You could even get up to 20 feet extra by using this technique.

- **The follow-through**

    Lastly, plant your foot firmly and release the disc as you complete your throw. As you release the disc, you will enter the follow-through. The follow-through is easy as you let your arms and body follow through with the motion. During this stage, you will experience a spin or move towards the direction of the throw, so allow it so you can get your balance.

Learn to Release the Disc Flow and Low

A big part of throwing a disc in disc golf is the releasing part. Releasing the disc too early or late will impact your throw. Hence, it is crucial to get the perfect timing to get the best distance and angle for the throw. Here are some tips and tricks to learn how to release the disc better.

- **Keep the disc and forearm parallel.**

    Throwing a disc the right way starts before you even actually throw it. This means that you have to hold it well if you want to get a good disc flow. To preserve the release angle, you should have your forearm parallel to the disc.

- **Waist not wrist**

    You should also adjust the angle once it's time to throw adequately. The angle of your release is dictated by bending the waist, not the wrist. Many beginners make the mistake of adjusting their wrist. But the truth is that manipulating the wrist to get a better release angle will disrupt the disc being parallel with your forearm.

- **Maintain release angle through the throw**

    While you release the disc, bending your waist helps you get a better angle. You should maintain that bent angle as you follow through with the throw. Hence, you must commit to the entire throw, which involves a follow-through.

Practice, Practice, and Practice

Remember, practice makes perfect. While reading this book gives you the necessary knowledge to go from having no clue about playing disc golf to playing a tournament, you wouldn't be able to compete with anyone if you do not practice. Practice helps you understand your body. As you know, practicing is all about repetition, and muscle memory comes in handy while competing in this game. While you practice, you can experiment with different discs, throws, and techniques to help you improve yourself.

A good rule of thumb for practicing disc golf is to practice something every day. However, while you are at it, ensure you do not get burnt out. Hence, you want to establish a schedule or routine. Also, your practice session does not have to be boring. A quick 20 to 30 minutes workout routine can help out your game. Also, when you go out to practice, you want to start by learning how to drive, and then learn about how to approach, and finally, learn how to putt.

Challenge Yourself: Play with Experienced Players

Many beginners in disc golf often shy away from playing with experienced players. They feel it's obvious they will lose, so why bother trying. But on the contrary, there are several reasons why you should try. One good reason to play with an experienced player is that you would pick up a couple of reasons why such a player is good at the game.

Another reason is that the experienced player can exploit your weak point. Perhaps you didn't even know you had such a weak point before the game. Hence, you will know areas you have mastered and need to work on. So, if you want to speed up the learning process, then practice with experienced players.

Keep it Simple

Playing disc golf does not necessarily need to be complex. You can keep your playing strategy as simple as possible and still be the game victor. However, you should still pay attention to the details of the game, such as release angle, throwing strength, stance, and so on. Also, don't worry too much about your throwing distance at first; keep your mind on mastering the technique. It is better to learn how to play disc golf with the right techniques and then build on your power than to learn with the wrong technique simply to get more power. Because at the end of the day, it is harder to unlearn a habit, which might make things harder for you down the line.

Last but not least, have fun.

Finally, don't get so carried away with winning without having fun playing the game. The whole idea of playing disc golf in the first place is to have fun. If you are too focused on the rules and applying one strategy, you will end up not having fun. This does not mean you should ignore every rule in the book; rather, you should have it at the back of your mind and not let it rule your mind.

Conclusion

Conclusively, playing disc golf is fun for everyone, both old and young. We wrote this book intending to help all disc golf players, including those who have no idea about the sport. Now that you have completed this book, one thing is sure: you have more knowledge about the game than you did before you started reading this book.

The ball is now in your court, as you can utilize this information as you please. But our advice is that you build on it and do so fast. Developing your disc golf-playing skills depends on how invested you are in practicing it. So, practice again, as you can never practice enough.

Made in United States
Troutdale, OR
07/02/2025